EVOLVE

WORKBOOK

Mari Vargo

3A

CAMBRIDGE
UNIVERSITY PRESS

Shaftesbury Road, Cambridge CB2 8EA, United Kingdom

One Liberty Plaza, 20th Floor, New York, NY 10006, USA

477 Williamstown Road, Port Melbourne, VIC 3207, Australia

314–321, 3rd Floor, Plot 3, Splendor Forum, Jasola District Centre, New Delhi – 110025, India

103 Penang Road, #05-06/07, Visioncrest Commercial, Singapore 238467

Cambridge University Press & Assessment is a department of the University of Cambridge.

We share the University's mission to contribute to society through the pursuit of education, learning and research at the highest international levels of excellence.

www.cambridge.org
Information on this title: www.cambridge.org/9781108408721

First published 2019

20 19 18 17 16 15 14 13 12 11 10 9 8 7

Printed in Poland by Opolgraf

A catalogue record for this publication is available from the British Library

ISBN 978-1-108-40527-0 Student's Book
ISBN 978-1-108-40507-2 Student's Book A
ISBN 978-1-108-40920-9 Student's Book B
ISBN 978-1-108-40528-7 Student's Book with Practice Extra
ISBN 978-1-108-40508-9 Student's Book with Practice Extra A
ISBN 978-1-108-40921-6 Student's Book with Practice Extra B
ISBN 978-1-108-40900-1 Workbook with Audio
ISBN 978-1-108-40872-1 Workbook with Audio A
ISBN 978-1-108-41193-6 Workbook with Audio B
ISBN 978-1-108-40517-1 Teacher's Edition with Test Generator
ISBN 978-1-108-41068-7 Presentation Plus
ISBN 978-1-108-41203-2 Class Audio CDs
ISBN 978-1-108-40793-9 Video Resource Book with DVD
ISBN 978-1-108-41447-0 Full Contact with DVD
ISBN 978-1-108-41154-7 Full Contact A with DVD
ISBN 978-1-108-41415-9 Full Contact B with DVD

Additional resources for this publication at www.cambridge.org/evolve

CONTENTS

1 VOCABULARY: Describing personality

A **Read a woman's descriptions of three people she knows. Then check (✓) <u>three</u> words that describe each person.**

1 My friend Anna is always in a good mood and spends a lot of time with friends. She doesn't get upset about little problems like missing the bus or losing her keys. But she's usually about 30 minutes late when we get together because she can't find her keys!

☑ cheerful ☐ nervous ☐ easygoing ☐ sociable ☐ reliable

2 Marco is eight years older than me. He's my brother, but sometimes he's more like a parent. He gives me money when I need it for rent or food. He gave me a room in his house when I first started school. He even protected me from our neighbor's angry dog when I was little. He's great, but he doesn't always tell me the truth. I mean, he never tells me when he has a problem. He doesn't want me to worry.

☐ brave ☐ generous ☐ honest ☐ selfish ☐ helpful

3 My friend James is the smartest person I know. He reads one or two books a week. I don't see him very often because he's always at home reading or studying. When we get together, we have interesting conversations about science and politics. I like talking with him, but some people don't feel the same way because he always tells them when they say something that's wrong.

☐ easygoing ☐ intelligent ☐ nervous ☐ serious ☐ honest

B **Describe yourself. Use the personality words from exercise 1A.**

_____

_____

_____

2 GRAMMAR: Information questions

A **Put the words in the correct order to write questions. Then match the questions with the answers.**

1 you / do / work / kind of / What / do / ?   <u>d</u>
  <u>What kind of work do you do?</u>

2 you / Why / Japanese / are / learning / ?   _____
  _____

3 teacher / your / Who's / Japanese / ?   _____
  _____

4 do / in / Which / you / live / neighborhood / ?   _____
  _____

5 is / next / When / class / your / ?   _____
  _____

6 class / in / are / history / you / Whose / ?   _____
  _____

a It's Professor Kubota.
b Professor King's class.
c It's at 2:00.
d I'm a nurse.
e I'm going to Japan this summer.
f I live near the university.

3 GRAMMAR AND VOCABULARY

A **Imagine a new student has just joined your class, and you want to find out about his or her personality. What questions can you ask? Complete the questions with your own ideas.**

1 What is the most _____ ?
2 Where do you love to _____ ?
3 How do you feel when _____ ?
4 When was the last time you _____ ?
5 Who do you spend _____ ?
6 Why _____ ?

B **Answer the questions from exercise 3A with true information.**

1 _____
2 _____
3 _____
4 _____
5 _____
6 _____

1.2 TRUE FRIENDS?

1 VOCABULARY: Giving personal information

A **Complete the sentences with the words and phrases in the box.**

am into	are married	are single	celebrate
live alone	live with my family	was born	was raised

1 I _____ in the 1980s. My birthday is June 18, 1984.

2 I _____ in a big city. I loved growing up in Hong Kong.

3 Both of my brothers _____. I don't have any sisters-in-law.

4 My best friend and I _____ to two amazing men. Now our husbands are friends, too.

5 I _____. I can't have my own apartment until I get a job.

6 I think it's fun to _____. I can sing out loud and no one can hear me.

7 I _____ video games. Sometimes I play them all night long.

8 I usually _____ my birthday with my family. We usually go out to dinner and have cake at home.

2 GRAMMAR: Indirect questions

A **Complete the conversation with the questions and answers in the box.**

> Do you know where she was born?
> I want to find out what kinds of things she's into.
> ~~Can you tell me what movies she was in?~~
> I wonder how old she is.
> I wonder if she lives with her family.

A I'm reading about the actress Hailee Steinfeld. Do you like her?

B I don't know. ¹Can you tell me what movies she was in? _____

A She was in *The Edge of Seventeen* and *Pitch Perfect 2*.

B Oh, yeah. I like her. ² _____

A She was born in 1996, so she's the same age as you.

B ³ _____

A I think she was born in California.

B ⁴ _____

A I don't know. I think she lives alone. ⁵ _____

B Well, we know she's into singing.

A Do you know if she's in a new movie?

B I don't know. Let's find out …

4

B   **Complete an indirect question for each answer. Include the correct punctuation – a period or a question mark. Remember: Do not use *do/does* in indirect questions.**

1   A   Do you know _____ *how old he is?* _____
    B   He's 20 years old.

2   A   Can you tell me _____
    B   He's into baseball.

3   A   I wonder _____
    B   He was born in Pusan, South Korea.

4   A   Do you know _____
    B   He was raised in Seoul.

5   A   I'd like to know _____
    B   He lives with his family.

3   GRAMMAR AND VOCABULARY

A   **Imagine you are having a conversation with a friend about a famous person. Complete the indirect questions. Then write responses to the questions. You can make up information about the famous person or check on the internet.**

Choose the famous person:

_____

Find out how old the person is.

A   Do you know ¹ _____ *when* _____ he/she ² _____ ?
B   _____

Ask where the person lived as a child.

A   I wonder ³ _____ he/she ⁴ _____ .
B   _____

Find out if the person is single or married.

A   I'd like to know ⁵ _____ he/she ⁶ _____ .
B   _____

1.3 NICE TALKING TO YOU

1 FUNCTIONAL LANGUAGE: Making introductions, saying how you know someone, and ending a conversation

A Put each sentence in the correct place in the chart.

> I work with Tony.
> ~~This is Maria, my wife.~~
> It was really nice to meet you.
>
> I'm Sonia.
> It was nice talking to you.
> How do you know Ivan?

Introductions	Saying how you know someone	Ending a conversation
This is Maria, my wife.		

B Complete the conversation using sentences from exercise 1A. You do not need to use all of the sentences.

A Hi! [1]_____ .

B Nice to meet you. So, [2]_____ ?

A Well, we worked together when we were in college.

B Cool. Oh wow, it's getting late. [3]_____ .

A It was good talking to you, too.

2 REAL-WORLD STRATEGY: Meeting someone you've heard about

A Put the conversations in order.

Conversation 1

It's nice to meet you, Brian. I've heard good things about you. _____

Hello. I'm Andy. I work with Tina. _____

Oh, that's nice. _____

Hi, Andy. I'm Brian. I'm Tina's brother. _____

Conversation 2

Hi, Ken. I'm Luis. It's nice to meet you. I've heard a lot about you. _____

Yes, only good things! _____

Hi, I'm Ken. I'm Tina's husband. _____

Good things, I hope! _____

6

3 FUNCTIONAL LANGUAGE AND REAL-WORLD STRATEGY

A **Read the information. Then complete the conversations with the correct words and phrases in the box.**

Conversation 1

Daniel is Heather's husband.

Heather and Tom are in school together.

| I've heard good things about you! | in my English class | ~~my husband~~ | Oh, that's nice. |

Heather Hi, Tom. This is Daniel, [1]_____my husband_____. Daniel, this is Tom.
He is [2]_____.

Daniel Hi, Tom. It's great to meet you. [3]_____

Tom [4]_____ I've heard good things about you, too!

Conversation 2

Vincent is Laurie's brother.   Carlo works with Vincent.

Julia is Carlo's wife.   Laurie is married to Sam.

| husband | wife | Good things I hope! |
| work with | sister | I've heard a lot about you! |

Carlo Hi, I'm Carlo. I [5]_____ Vincent. How do you know him?

Laurie Hi, Carlo. I'm Laurie, Vincent's [6]_____.

Carlo [7]_____

Laurie [8]_____

Carlo Yes, only good things! This is my [9]_____, Julia.

Laurie Hi, Julia. It's so nice to meet you. This is my [10]_____, Sam.

B **Now imagine you are at a party with a friend, and you see a classmate. Introduce them. Have them say that they've heard about each other. Then end the conversation.**

You Hi, _____! How nice to see you here! This is my friend, _____.

Friend _____.

Classmate Hi, _____. _____

Friend _____

Classmate _____

Friend _____

Classmate _____

You _____

WE'RE FAMILY!

1 READING

A **READ FOR DETAIL** Read the email. Then read the statements and check (✓) *True*, *False*, or *Not given*.

To: ericanyc@cup.org

From: ditamx@cup.org

Subject: Info about Boston

Hi Erica,

My name is Dita. I live in Mexico City. You work with my sister, Belen, in New York. She gave me your email address. I hope that's OK. I'm writing because I want to go to Boston, Massachusetts, next summer, and I'd like to find out more about it. Belen told me that you were raised in Boston. Can you tell me a little bit about the city?

I'm wondering what the weather is like in Boston in the summer. I'd also like to find out how much money I need. Do you know how much an apartment in the city costs? My friend Marta wants to come, too. She wants to live with me, so we need a two-bedroom apartment.

Marta and I are both into music. Do you know if there are any good places to listen to music? Can you tell me if there are big concert halls in Boston? What else can we do there?

Hope to hear from you soon.

Dita

		True	False	Not given
1	Dita lives in New York.	☐	☑	☐
2	Belen works in New York.	☐	☐	☐
3	Erica was born in Boston.	☐	☐	☐
4	Dita wants to go to Boston.	☐	☐	☐
5	Belen goes to school with Erica.	☐	☐	☐
6	Dita works at an office in Mexico City.	☐	☐	☐

2 LISTENING

A 🔊 **1.01** Listen to the conversation and (circle) the correct answers.

1 Erica is talking to _____ .
   a Dita   **(b)** Belen   c Marta

2 Erica _____ Dita's email.
   a read   b answered   c didn't get

3 Erica says that Boston is _____ .
   a an expensive city   b a safe city   c a busy place

4 Boston has a lot of _____ .
   a sports teams   b rain   c colleges

A   Imagine Dita is asking you about your city. Reply to her email. Write paragraphs about your city.

Hi, Dita.

It was great to hear from you. _____

_____

_____

_____

_____

_____

_____

_____

_____

CHECK AND REVIEW

Read the statements. Can you do these things?

UNIT 1	Mark the boxes. ☑ I can do it. [?] I am not sure. I can …	If you are not sure, go back to these pages in the Student's Book.
VOCABULARY	☐ use adjectives to describe personality. ☐ use words to give personal information.	page 2 page 4
GRAMMAR	☐ ask information questions. ☐ use indirect questions.	page 3 page 5
FUNCTIONAL LANGUAGE	☐ make introductions and say how you know someone. ☐ meet someone you've heard about.	page 6 page 7
SKILLS	☐ use paragraphs in an email. ☐ use different opening and closing sentences in an email.	page 9 page 9

1   VOCABULARY: Describing possessions

A   **Find 11 more vocabulary words or phrases in the word search.**

M	O	D	C	G	M	N	I	D	L	V	U	A	I	Z
B	U	S	E	F	U	L	U	G	O	T	M	N	N	P
Y	B	O	N	W	R	F	P	C	V	B	X	L	G	M
T	R	S	A	Y	C	N	S	I	C	O	M	M	O	N
U	A	G	M	O	D	E	R	N	C	U	P	T	O	K
D	N	F	D	D	A	L	O	I	F	G	Z	U	D	T
U	D	O	T	T	M	N	M	A	B	D	Y	S	C	G
S	N	P	I	X	A	D	G	D	M	L	N	E	O	U
C	E	V	N	A	G	C	U	S	O	O	T	L	N	L
P	W	A	C	I	E	O	U	T	D	A	T	E	D	A
X	O	M	F	B	D	L	V	Z	A	F	C	S	I	C
U	P	T	G	M	H	F	A	N	C	Y	U	S	T	U
S	P	E	C	I	A	L	E	N	K	D	S	M	I	C
E	C	R	D	R	A	H	C	I	U	B	P	G	O	V
D	B	T	O	D	U	M	F	L	P	L	A	I	N	I

brand new
common
damaged
fancy
in good condition
modern
outdated
plain
special
useless
~~useful~~
used

B   **Complete the sentences with the words and phrases in the box.**

> brand new   in good condition   outdated   special   useless

1   My comic books might be worth a lot of money some day, so I keep them in a
    _____ box.
2   This sweater is _____ . I just bought it yesterday.
3   I need a new phone. Mine is really _____ .
4   Don't throw that bike away. It's still _____ . You can sell it.
5   I don't know why I still have this broken printer. It's _____ .

2   GRAMMAR: Present perfect with *ever, never, for,* and *since*

A   Circle *ever, never, for,* or *since* to complete each sentence.
1   I've had this phone *ever / never /* (for)*/ since* three years.
2   Have you known Mike *ever / never / for / since* a long time?
3   These old computer games have *ever / never / for / since* worked!
4   You haven't been here *ever / never / for / since* last year.
5   Have your friends *ever / never / for / since* given you something really special?
6   We've ridden the same bikes *ever / never / for / since* years.
7   He's lived here *ever / never / for / since* 2015.

B   **Complete the conversations. Use the present perfect forms of the verbs in parentheses ( ). Use *for* or *since* in the answers.**

1   A   How long _____have_____ you _____had_____ these shoes? (have)

    B   I _____ them _____ a long time. (have)

2   A   _____ you ever _____ this guitar? (play)

    B   Yes, I _____ guitar lessons _____ I was ten years old. (take)

3   A   How long _____ this television _____ damaged? (be)

    B   It _____ damaged _____ last year. (be)

4   A   _____ you _____ this bike recently? (use)

    B   No, I _____ it _____ about a year. (use)

5   A   How long _____ your brother _____ this car? (have)

    B   He _____ it _____ he finished college. (own)

3   GRAMMAR AND VOCABULARY

A   **Complete the chart with your own ideas. Write two more phrases for each verb.**

have	ride	play
have shoes	ride a bike	play *computer games*

own	watch	collect
own souvenirs	watch a DVD	collect _____

B   **Write questions with *Have you ever* and phrases from the chart in exercise 3A.**

1   Have you ever played computer games? _____

2   _____

3   _____

4   _____

5   _____

6   _____

C   **Write answers to the questions from exercise 3B. Use *never*, *for*, or *since* and add details.**

1   I haven't played computer games since I was in first grade. _____

2   _____

3   _____

4   _____

5   _____

6   _____

2.2 SO MANY FEATURES

1 VOCABULARY: Tech features

A **Match the two parts of the sentences to complete the definitions.**

1 A **device** is _____
2 If you **delete** something, _____
3 A **folder** is _____
4 Your **home screen** is _____
5 A **model** of something is _____
6 If you **set** something **up**, _____
7 The **storage** on a computer is _____
8 If you **sync** a phone to a computer, _____
9 If you **try** something, _____
10 If something **works**, _____

a you make it ready to use.
b you match the two things so they have the same information.
c you erase or remove it from a computer.
d one type of that thing, such as a phone or a car.
e it functions well, or it is successful.
f the screen you see when you start using your phone or computer.
g something you use for doing a special job.
h you use it for the first time to see what it is like.
i a place on a computer or phone where you organize files and apps.
j the space where a computer saves everything, including photos, music, and apps.

2 GRAMMAR: Present perfect with *already* and *yet*

A **Complete each sentence with *already* or *yet*.**

1 Have you set up your new laptop _____ ?
2 I haven't finished my homework _____ .
3 Stella has _____ deleted the email.
4 Lee hasn't called me _____ .
5 We've _____ bought new phones.

B **Find one mistake in each sentence. Then rewrite the sentence correctly.**

1 She's taken already that computer class.

_____

2 Have yet you used your new laptop?

_____

3 We haven't seen the new model already.

_____

4 He's set up already his phone.

_____

5 I've downloaded that song yet, but I'm going to later.

_____

A   Read Mark's and Tina's to-do lists. What things have they finished? What do they still have to do? Write sentences using the present perfect with *already* or *yet*.

Mark's To-Do List

✓ set up my new phone

  sync all my devices

✓ delete folders on my home screen

✓ try my new apps

  buy more storage for my computer

Tina's To-Do List

✓ set up my new phone

  sync all my devices

✓ delete folders on my home screen

  change the picture on my home screen

✓ delete old emails

1 They've already set up their new phones.

2 They _____

3 They _____

4 Mark _____

5 Tina _____

6 Mark _____

7 Tina _____

B   Write your to-do list from yesterday. Check (✓) two things you've already done. Leave one thing you haven't done yet.

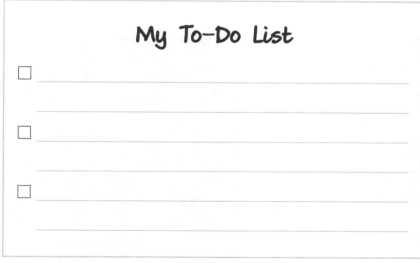

My To-Do List

☐ _____

☐ _____

☐ _____

C   Write sentences about your notes in exercise 3B. Use *already* and *yet*.

1 _____

2 _____

3 _____

2.3 GUESS WHAT?

1 FUNCTIONAL LANGUAGE: Introducing topics, changing the subject, and staying on track

A **Complete the conversation with the correct words and phrases.**

> anyway   by the way   guess what   oh, before I forget   ~~you know~~

A It's so good to see you, Ed!

B Yeah, I haven't seen you in a long time, Misha! What's new?

A Well, ¹_____*you know*_____ I was looking for a bigger apartment because I have so much stuff.

B Yes, I remember. Did you move?

A Not yet, but ²_____? My building manager quit last month, and I'm the new manager!

B Congratulations! I hope you're a nice apartment manager!

A Of course! ³_____, I have to work more now, but I can have a bigger apartment.

B I'm so happy for you. ⁴_____, my sister asked me to say "hello" to you.

A That's nice. Tell her I said, "hi," too. How is she?

B She's great. ⁵_____, I saw your brother at school last week. He's in my English class.

A Really? I didn't know that!

2 REAL-WORLD STRATEGY: Using short questions to show interest

A **Put the conversation in order.**

A I went to Los Angeles last weekend with my sister.   `1`

B She did? What did she buy?   _____

B You are? Why do you want to go back?   _____

A Yeah, we had a great time, but it's really expensive there.   _____

A Well, we went shopping. My sister bought a lot of stuff.   _____

A My sister wants to return all her dresses and shoes!   _____

A A few dresses and five pairs of shoes. We're planning to go back next month.   _____

B Really? Did you have fun?   _____

B It is? What did you do that cost so much money?   _____

3 FUNCTIONAL LANGUAGE AND REAL-WORLD STRATEGY

A **Find and correct <u>three</u> errors in each conversation.**

Conversation 1

A You know I collect old toy cars, right?

B You did? I didn't know that.

A Yeah, I do, and guess where? I found a box full of toy cars in my uncle's garage!

B You were? Wow, that's great!

A I know, and they're in really good condition, too.

Conversation 2

A My roommate and I cleaned our apartment last weekend, and we gave away a bunch of stuff.

B You are? What did you give away?

A Mostly clothes and books. By the was, I found your sweater. You left it at my house.

B I was? When did I leave it there?

A I think you left it last week. I can bring it to class tomorrow.

B Thanks.

B **Complete the conversation with your own ideas. Use phrases to introduce new topics, change the subject, and stay on track. Include short questions to show interest.**

A So, you know I like to go to garage sales.

B Yeah, you always find a lot of really cool old stuff.

A That's right. Well, [1]_____?
I found [2]_____ yesterday!

B [3]_____? Where did you find it?

A It was [4]_____.

B [5]_____? How much did you pay for it?

A Kind of a lot. The guy wanted
[6]_____ for it.

B Wow! How much do you think it's actually worth?

A It's worth about [7]_____! Oh, sorry, my phone is ringing.

B That's OK.

A Hmm ... It's a wrong number. [8]_____,
isn't that amazing?

B Yeah, it is. By the way, I want to go with you next time!

A Of course! Why don't you come with me on Sunday?

IT'S USELESS, RIGHT?

1 LISTENING

A 🔊 **2.01** **LISTEN FOR DETAIL** Listen to the conversation. Read each statement and write *T* (true) or *F* (false).

1 James is at Kevin's house. _____

2 Kevin's dad collected a lot of different things. _____

3 Kevin's dad wants Kevin to organize everything and give it away. _____

4 James can help Kevin because he isn't busy today. _____

5 James agrees that Kevin should give everything away. _____

B 🔊 **2.01** Listen to the conversation again. Circle the correct answers.

1 What did Kevin's dad collect?

   a coins, stamps, and watches   **b** books, coins, and baseball cards   **c** watches and chairs

2 What does Kevin have to do?

   a sell everything online   **b** put everything in the garage   **c** count everything

3 What is worth $500?

   a a coin   **b** a book   **c** a baseball card

4 How does James find the price?

   a He looks in a book.   **b** He looks online.   **c** He asks Kevin's dad.

2 READING

A Read Kevin's notes for his first ad. Then circle the best ad for this item.

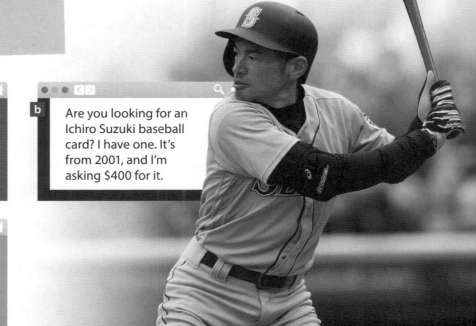

baseball card   2001
Ichiro Suzuki   signed on front
Seattle Mariners $400
Good condition

a I'm selling a baseball card. It is in good condition and is signed on the front. Suzuki played for the Seattle Mariners.

b Are you looking for an Ichiro Suzuki baseball card? I have one. It's from 2001, and I'm asking $400 for it.

c This Ichiro Suzuki baseball card is in good condition. It is from 2001 and has Suzuki's signature on the front. $400

WRITING

A   **Think of something that you want to sell. What does the item look like? Make notes and suggest a price.**

Condition: _____

Age: _____

Color: _____

Other: _____

Price: _____

B   **Use the information from exercise 3A to write an ad for your item. Use *one* and *ones* to avoid repetition.**

CHECK AND REVIEW

Read the statements. Can you do these things?

UNIT 2	Mark the boxes. ☑ I can do it. ? I am not sure. I can ...	If you are not sure, go back to these pages in the Student's Book.
VOCABULARY	☐ describe possessions.	page 12
	☐ talk about tech features.	page 14
GRAMMAR	☐ use the present perfect with *ever, never, for,* and *since*.	page 13
	☐ use the present perfect with *already* and *yet*.	page 15
FUNCTIONAL LANGUAGE	☐ introduce topics, change the subject, and stay on track.	page 16
	☐ use short questions to show interest.	page 17
SKILLS	☐ write an ad for something I want to sell.	page 19
	☐ use *one* and *ones* to avoid repetition.	page 19

1   VOCABULARY: City features

A   **Put the words in the correct places in the chart.**

| bridge | clinic | embassy | ferry | fire station | highway |
| hostel | monument | parking lot | sidewalk | sculpture | tunnel |

Buildings where people work	Things related to transportation	Other

2   GRAMMAR: Articles

A   **Match each sentence with the correct rule.**

1   He's at the airport. _____

2   I don't like milk. _____

3   My brother is a doctor. _____

a   Don't use an article when you talk about something in general.

b   Use *a/an* to talk about singular nouns.

c   Use *the* with something your listener already knows about.

B   **Complete the sentences with the words and phrases in the box. Add *a*, *an*, or *the* where necessary.**

| bank | grocery store | Madrid | Pine Street | tallest building | trains |

1   I live in _____, but I didn't grow up in the city.

2   Is there _____ near here? I need to get some money.

3   Buses are slower than _____.

4   I think my friend lives on _____.

5   That's _____ in town – it has 40 floors.

6   Can you please get some milk at _____?

C **Circle *a, an, the,* or Ø (no article).**

1 We saw *a* / *an* / *the* / Ø beautiful monument today. I don't know what it's called.

2 I think *a* / *an* / *the* / Ø Tokyo is the most exciting city in the world.

3 I'm looking for *a* / *an* / *the* / Ø apartment downtown.

4 We're not far from *a* / *an* / *the* / Ø hotel. You can go get a jacket from your room.

5 Close *a* / *an* / *the* / Ø door. It's cold.

6 *A* / *An* / *The* / Ø last train leaves at midnight.

7 *A* / *An* / *The* / Ø best shops are on *a* / *an* / *the* / Ø Jones Street.

8 Have you ever been to *a* / *an* / *the* / Ø Kings Park in *a* / *an* / *the* / Ø Australia?

3 GRAMMAR AND VOCABULARY

A **Complete each question with a noun or noun phrase in the box and the correct article (or no article).**

bridges	clinic	hostels	monuments	most beautiful sculpture	parking lot

1 What is _____ in your city? Where is it? Who is the artist?

2 If you're sick, is there _____ nearby that you can go to?

3 Are there any _____ or cheap hotels in your city where travelers can stay?

4 Are there any _____ in town? Are they for driving on or for walking on?

5 Where can we leave our car? Is there _____ by the movie theater?

6 Does your city have any _____ or other landmarks? What are they for?

B **Now answer the questions in exercise 3A about your city.**

1 _____
_____
_____

2 _____
_____
_____

3 _____
_____
_____

4 _____
_____
_____

5 _____
_____
_____

6 _____
_____
_____

3.2 A MAP LIKE SPAGHETTI

1 VOCABULARY: Public transportation

A Unscramble the letters to make words related to public transportation.

1 arfe _____
2 lein _____
3 oobk _____
4 otuer _____
5 recdit _____

6 rrivlaa _____
7 maltinre _____
8 duchslee _____
9 uparreetd _____
10 otnrreesavi _____

B Complete the travel agent's web page with words from exercise 1A. You do not need four of the words.

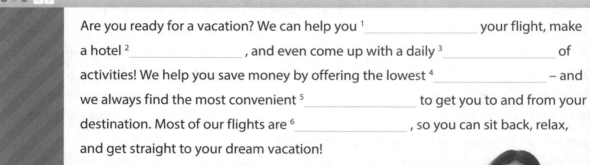

Are you ready for a vacation? We can help you [1]_____ your flight, make a hotel [2]_____ , and even come up with a daily [3]_____ of activities! We help you save money by offering the lowest [4]_____ – and we always find the most convenient [5]_____ to get you to and from your destination. Most of our flights are [6]_____ , so you can sit back, relax, and get straight to your dream vacation!

2 GRAMMAR: Modals for advice

A Put the conversation in the correct order.

A When should we book them? _____
B I'd book tickets online. _____
A Would you take a bus to the city? ___1___
A OK. Thanks. _____
B I'd take the 9:00 train. _____
A Which train would you take? _____
B No, I wouldn't. I'd take a train. _____
A How can we book our tickets? _____
B You could book them right now. Here, use my phone. _____

B **Complete the conversations with modals for advice and the verbs in parentheses ( ). Different answers are possible.**

1 A You [1]_____could take_____ a bus. (take)

   B Which bus [2]_____ I [3]_____ ? (take)

   A Well, I usually take the cross-town express bus.

2 A You [4]_____ by ferry. (go)

   B OK. How [5]_____ I [6]_____ my ticket? (book)

   A Just buy a ticket at the terminal.

3 A You and your friend [7]_____ to the airport too late. (not / get)

   B When [8]_____ we [9]_____ ? (leave)

   A At least three hours before your flight.

4 A Which train [10]_____ we [11]_____ to the park? (take)

   B You [12]_____ to the park. It's not far. (walk)

3 GRAMMAR AND VOCABULARY

A **Complete the instructions with words in the box and modals for advice.**

| arrival | direct | fare | line | schedule | terminal |

From: Monica Martin

To: Sarah Jong

Subject: How to get to my place

Hey, Sarah!

I'm so glad that you're coming to visit me next month. I know it's your first time flying, so here are some tips:

First, you [1]_____ book a [2]_____ flight so you don't have to stop anywhere on the way. I [3]_____ get a flight with an early [4]_____ because I have to work until 5:00. You [5]_____ take a taxi here, but I [6]_____ take the train. A train ticket is much cheaper than a taxi [7]_____ . You can get to the train station from any [8]_____ in the airport. You [9]_____ take the L, M, or N [10]_____ . You [11]_____ check the train [12]_____ to see what time the trains leave and pick the best one. You [13]_____ get off the train at the 9th Street or 10th Street station. My apartment is between the two stations.

I can't wait to see you!

xo,

Monica

UP AND DOWN

1 FUNCTIONAL LANGUAGE: Asking for and giving directions

A **Match the sentence halves.**

1 Can you tell me how _____
2 Which way _____
3 Do you know which floor _____
4 How do I _____
5 It's on _____
6 Go down _____
7 Room 332 _____
8 It's downstairs _____

a meeting room 22 is on?
b the first hallway.
c to get to the elevator?
d in the lobby.
e is on your right.
f get to the main entrance?
g is room 332?
h the second floor.

2 REAL-WORLD STRATEGY: Repeating details to show you understand

A **Complete the conversations. Repeat details to show you understand.**

1 A Where's the closest restroom?
  B _____? It's down the hall on your right.

2 A Excuse me. Can you tell me how to get to the train station downtown?
  B _____? Sure, just go down Stark Avenue and it's on the left.

3 A I'm really hungry. Where's the cafeteria?
  B _____? It's in building B.

4 A Which way is the computer lab that has printers in it?
  B _____? It's upstairs on the third floor.

5 A Do you know which floor the main office is on?
  B _____? It's downstairs on the first floor.

FUNCTIONAL LANGUAGE AND REAL-WORLD STRATEGY

A **Imagine you work at your favorite restaurant or café. Complete the customers' questions using the phrases in the box. Give answers. Then write responses. Remember to repeat details to show you understand.**

> do I get to   way is the   you tell me where

Conversation 1

A Excuse me, which [1]_____ <u>nearest ATM?</u>

B Oh, just go out the front door and [2]_____ . But did you know you can pay with a credit card here?

A [3]_____

Conversation 2

A Can you help me? How [4]_____ <u>the bathroom?</u>

B Sure. It's [5]_____ . Do you see the sign that says "restrooms"?

A [6]_____

Conversation 3

A Sorry, but can [7]_____ the coat closet is? I'd like to hang up my jacket.

B Yes, it's [8]_____ . Wow, it's really raining out there! Would you like me to take your umbrella, too?

A [9]_____

B **Complete the questions about your home. Use the phrases in the box and the instructions in parentheses ( ). The phrases will be used more than once. Then answer the questions so they are true for you. Repeat details to show you understand.**

> Can you tell me how to get to   How do I get to   Which way is

1 A _____
   the kitchen? (from your living room)

   B _____
   _____

2 A _____
   the front door? (from your living room)

   B _____
   _____

3 A _____
   the bathroom? (from your kitchen)

   B _____
   _____

4 A _____
   the bedroom? (from the bathroom)

   B _____
   _____

5 A _____
   the living room? (from the bedroom)

   B _____

MAYBE YOU CAN HELP!

1 READING

A **READ FOR DETAIL** Read the ad. Then answer the questions.

> **The 25th Annual Cross-City 10K Race is happening on May 27** – join the race or volunteer!

> **RUN**
The race route will take runners through the whole city. The race starts at the ferry terminal and ends at the soccer field in Miller Park. Sign up for the race online. The deadline to sign up is May 15. Click here to sign up.

> **WATCH**
Stand along the race route and cheer the runners on. After the race, stay and enjoy free food and drinks and a concert in the park. Click here to see the concert schedule.

> **VOLUNTEER**
Several of our runners are coming from out of town. A couple of days before the race, we need volunteers to meet them at the airport or the train station and tell them which buses or trains to take to get to their hotels. These volunteers will also give runners race information, schedules, and directions to the race's starting line. On race day, volunteers will stand on the race route and hand out water to all of the runners.

Volunteers should have a lot of energy, enjoy meeting new people, and know how to get around the city. Click here to volunteer.

1 What is the ad about?

2 What are three things that volunteers will have to do?

3 What three characteristics should volunteers have?

2 LISTENING

A 🔊 3.01 Listen to the conversation. Circle the correct answers to the questions.

1 What does Anna want to do?

  a run   **b** volunteer

2 What does Robin want to do?

  a run   **b** volunteer

3 Why does Anna know the city well?

  a She's lived there for a long time.   **b** She goes to school in the city.

4 Why doesn't Robin know the city well?

  a She doesn't go out very much.   **b** She moved there a few months ago.

5 Has Robin ever run in a race?

  a yes   **b** no

3 WRITING

A Imagine you want to be a volunteer for the race in exercise 1A. Complete the application.
Then check your punctuation and grammar.

1 Why do you want to be a volunteer?

_____

_____

2 Have you ever volunteered for anything before?

_____

_____

3 Why do you think you would be a good volunteer?

_____

_____

4 Do you like meeting new people? Why or why not?

_____

_____

5 Do you know the city well? Write directions from one place in the city to another place.

_____

_____

_____

CHECK AND REVIEW

Read the statements. Can you do these things?

UNIT 3	Mark the boxes. ☑ I can do it. ? I am not sure. I can …	If you are not sure, go back to these pages in the Student's Book.
VOCABULARY	☐ identify different features in my city. ☐ talk about traveling and using public transportation.	page 22 page 24
GRAMMAR	☐ use articles correctly. ☐ use modals to give advice.	page 23 page 25
FUNCTIONAL LANGUAGE	☐ ask for and give directions. ☐ repeat details to show I understand.	page 26 page 27
SKILLS	☐ complete an application. ☐ check my own writing for accuracy and correct use of grammar and punctuation.	page 29 page 29

1   VOCABULARY: Describing opinions and reactions

A Complete the sentences with the words in the box. Add the correct ending (-ed or -ing) to each word.

amuse	annoy	disappoint	embarrass
fascinate	frighten	shock	surprise

1 It's so _____annoying_____ when people park in my parking space!
2 The movie was kind of funny. I was _____ , but I didn't really laugh out loud.
3 I forgot my wallet today, so I couldn't pay for my lunch. I had to borrow money from a co-worker. It was really _____ .
4 I'm _____ that I didn't get the job. I really wanted it.
5 I couldn't believe that I won a new car. I was _____ !
6 This book had a _____ ending. I expected it to end differently.
7 Tom loves to read about space exploration. He thinks it's _____ .
8 My sister never watches scary movies. She gets too _____ .

2   GRAMMAR: *be going to* and *will* for predictions

A Put the words in the correct order to write predictions.

1 get / work / He / won't / to / time / on / .
   He won't get to work on time.
2 she's / going / us / think / to / I / don't / with / come / .
   _____
3 to / great / going / We're / time / have / a / .
   _____
4 well / this / I'll / do / school / year / in / .
   _____
5 and / late / Mark / dinner / I / be / for / will / .
   _____
6 like / idea / He's / to / this / going / not / .
   _____

Rewrite the sentences from exercise 2A. Change *be going to* **to** *will* **and** *will* **to** *be going to.*

1 <u>He's not going to get to work on time.</u>

2 _____

3 _____

4 _____

5 _____

6 _____

3 GRAMMAR AND VOCABULARY

A **Complete the predictions with the correct form of the phrases in parentheses ( ) and the words in the box.**

amused	annoyed	disappointed	frightened	surprising

1 My son is scared of storms, and it ____is going to thunder____ tonight. (be going to / thunder)
  I hope he doesn't feel too _____ .

2 My mom _____ this funny photo. (will / love) She'll be so
  _____ !

3 Do you think your friends _____ really sad you can't go to the show? (be going
  to / be) I hope they aren't too _____ .

4 My travel app says the bus _____ 15 minutes late this morning. (will / arrive)
  I'm so _____ !

5 I don't think my boss _____ that I dyed my hair a different color. (will / care)
  Things like that aren't usually very _____ to her.

B **Complete the predictions with your own ideas. Use** *will* **or** *be going to.*

1 My parents ___are going to be___ surprised when ___I come home for my mother's birthday___ .

2 My _____ annoyed when _____
  _____ .

3 I don't think my _____ shocked when _____
  _____ .

4 It _____ frightening when _____
  _____ .

5 I think it _____ disappointing when _____
  _____ .

6 It _____ amusing when _____
  _____ .

1   VOCABULARY: Making decisions and plans

A   **Match the sentence halves.**

1 Let's arrange ___d___   a to bring your driver's license on the trip.
2 Don't forget _____   b the hotel reservations?
3 I'm going to meet up _____   c that we're going to be late?
4 Did you deal with _____   d a coffee date this week.
5 Can you let them know _____   e with some friends for dinner tonight.

B   **Complete the sentences with the phrases in the box.**

Can you check	How can I get in touch	I have to think about this
Let's look into	Please remind me	

1 ___How can I get in touch___ with you when you're on your trip?
2 _____ the weather on your phone?
3 _____ to buy our plane tickets tonight.
4 _____ before I make a decision.
5 _____ staying at a hotel near the beach.

2   GRAMMAR: *will* for sudden decisions; present continuous for future plans

A   **Choose the correct verb form to complete each question. Then answer the questions.**

1   A What *will you do /* (*are you doing*) this weekend?
     B I'm driving to the beach with my family.

2   A *Will you leave / Are you leaving* for your flight this afternoon?
     B _____

3   A Someone is at the door. *Will you see / Are you seeing* who it is?
     B _____

4   A *Will you take / Are you taking* a vacation in December?
     B _____

5   A It's too late for your parents to call now. *Will they call / Are they calling* tomorrow?
     B _____

6   A I don't want to cook tonight. *Will you buy / Are you buying* something for dinner on your way home?
     B _____

7   A It's the twins' birthday on Friday. *Will they have / Are they having* a dinner party?
     B _____

GRAMMAR AND VOCABULARY

A **Write answers to the questions with the words in parentheses ( ) and your own ideas. Write four sentences with *will* and four sentences with the present continuous.**

1   A   What are you doing this weekend?

    B   (meet up) I'm meeting up with John at the park on Saturday.

2   A   Are we getting close to the airport?

    B   (check) _____

3   A   I think we're going to be about ten minutes late. Sandra must be wondering where we are.

    B   (let Sandra know) _____

4   A   Have you seen Kevin lately?

    B   (get in touch) _____

5   A   Have you made hotel reservations yet?

    B   (deal with) _____

6   A   I hope I don't forget to pack all my chargers.

    B   (remind) _____

7   A   When can I talk to your boss about a job?

    B   (arrange) _____

8   A   Do you want to go to the movies Friday night?

    B   (think about) _____

9   A   Do you know where you're going for your vacation?

    B   (look into) _____

4.3 A DRIVING TEST

1 FUNCTIONAL LANGUAGE: Offering and responding to reassurance

A **Complete the conversations with the sentences in the box.**

> I hope so.
> I really appreciate it.
> There's no need to worry.
> He'll be fine.
> Thanks, but I feel so bad.
> ~~It's no problem.~~
> Don't worry about the clothes.

Conversation 1

A I'm so sorry that I broke your coffee mug.

B ¹ It's no problem.   I didn't really like that mug, anyway.

A ² _____

B It's OK. These things happen sometimes.

Conversation 2

A I'm so worried.

B ³ _____

A But it looked like Alan really hurt himself.

B ⁴ _____ The doctors will take good care of him.

A ⁵ _____

Conversation 3

A I'm so sorry I dropped your scarf and hat in that puddle yesterday.

B ⁶ _____ I'm just glad you got home before the streets flooded!

A Me, too! And I'll buy you new ones this weekend.

B Thanks, ⁷ _____

2 REAL-WORLD STRATEGY: Using *at least* to point out the good side of a situation

A **Match the sentences.**

1 I have to work on Friday.   b   a At least it's not raining like it was yesterday.

2 I didn't get the job.   _____   b At least you have the weekend off.

3 It's so hot today.   _____   c At least you have two other interviews this week.

4 I didn't get all the classes that I wanted.   _____   d At least you were able to get most of them.

5 Someone broke my car window.   _____   e At least they didn't take anything.

FUNCTIONAL LANGUAGE AND REAL-WORLD STRATEGY

A   **Write a response to each statement with a sentence in the box. The sentences will be used more than once. Then write another response with *at least*. Add your own ideas.**

'll be fine.	Don't worry about it.
These things happen sometimes.	There's no need to worry.

1 **A** Someone crashed into my car yesterday, so I have to walk to work.
   B *It'll be fine. I walk to work every day, and it's not too bad.*
   C *At least you'll get some exercise.*

2 **A** We're late for the 7:00 movie.
   B _____
   C _____

3 **A** Oh no! I don't have any money, and it's my turn to pay for lunch.
   B _____
   C _____

4 **A** I forgot to invite Michael to my party. I think I hurt his feelings.
   B _____
   C _____

5 **A** I lost your sweater! I'm sorry!
   B _____
   C _____

6 **A** The refrigerator is too full.
   B _____
   C _____

7 **A** I failed my driving test.
   B _____
   C _____

1   LISTENING

A   🔊 **4.01**   **LISTEN FOR MAIN IDEAS**   **Listen to the conversation and check (✓) the <u>five</u> ideas that Sam and David discuss. Underline the idea that they agree on.**

- ☐ a party at Alex's house
- ☐ dinner at David's house
- ☐ a basketball game
- ☐ a day at the beach
- ☐ a party at the community center
- ☐ a concert
- ☐ dinner at a restaurant
- ☐ a party at the park

B   🔊 **4.01**   **LISTEN FOR DETAIL**   **Listen again and write the reasons they say "no" to four of the ideas and "yes" to one idea.**

1   First idea: _____

2   Second idea: _____

3   Third idea: _____

4   Fourth idea: _____

5   Fifth idea: _____

2   READING

A   **Read the invitation. Then answer the questions.**

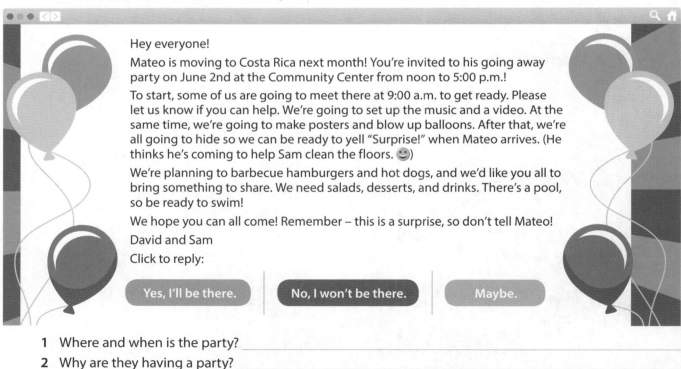

Hey everyone!

Mateo is moving to Costa Rica next month! You're invited to his going away party on June 2nd at the Community Center from noon to 5:00 p.m.!

To start, some of us are going to meet there at 9:00 a.m. to get ready. Please let us know if you can help. We're going to set up the music and a video. At the same time, we're going to make posters and blow up balloons. After that, we're all going to hide so we can be ready to yell "Surprise!" when Mateo arrives. (He thinks he's coming to help Sam clean the floors. 🙂)

We're planning to barbecue hamburgers and hot dogs, and we'd like you all to bring something to share. We need salads, desserts, and drinks. There's a pool, so be ready to swim!

We hope you can all come! Remember – this is a surprise, so don't tell Mateo!

David and Sam

Click to reply:

[Yes, I'll be there.]   [No, I won't be there.]   [Maybe.]

1   Where and when is the party? _____

2   Why are they having a party? _____

3   What three things do David and Sam want people to do?

- ■ Bring _____
- ■ Help _____
- ■ Don't _____

3 WRITING

A Imagine that you are going to have a surprise party for a friend's birthday. Complete the invitation.

Hey everyone!

You're invited to _____ 's birthday party! The party is going to be at _____ from _____ .

To start, some of us are going to meet at _____ on _____ to get ready. Please let us know if you can help.

We're going to _____ . At the same time, we're going to _____ . After that, we're all going to _____ .

We're planning to _____ , and we'd like you all to bring _____ .

We hope you can all come! Remember – this is a surprise, so don't tell _____ !

See you there,

_____

CHECK AND REVIEW

Read the statements. Can you do these things?

UNIT 4	Mark the boxes. ☑ I can do it. ❓ I am not sure. I can …	If you are not sure, go back to these pages in the Student's Book.
VOCABULARY	☐ use adjectives to describe opinions and reactions. ☐ use verbs and verb phrases for decisions and plans.	page 34 page 36
GRAMMAR	☐ use *be going to* and *will* for predictions. ☐ use *will* for sudden decisions and present continuous for future plans.	page 35 page 37
FUNCTIONAL LANGUAGE	☐ offer reassurance. ☐ respond to reassurance with *at least*.	page 38 page 39
SKILLS	☐ write an email describing plans for an event. ☐ use linking words to show the order of events.	page 41 page 41

1   VOCABULARY: Losing and finding things

A   **Circle the correct words to complete the story.**

Can you imagine losing something and having it [1]*appear*/ *disappear* again a quarter of a century later? April Bolt can. Twenty-five years ago, Bolt [2]*left her purse behind / got her purse back* on a boat on South Carolina's Lake Hartwell. Before she could go back to get it, it [3]*appeared / disappeared*. Maybe it [4]*fell off / dropped* the boat. Or maybe someone picked it up and [5]*fell off / dropped* it in the lake. She [6]*searched for / located* it, but couldn't find it. Just a few months ago, however, 11-year-old Brodie Brooks [7]*discovered / searched for* it while he was fishing on the same lake with his family. When Brooks opened the purse and found the owner's driver's license, his relative Ben Myers recognized the woman in the photo. She was a family friend! Myers [8]*returned / located* Bolt and [9]*left behind / returned* her purse to her. She was shocked that someone found it and was happy to [10]*get it back / leave it behind*.

2   GRAMMAR: Simple past

A   **Write the affirmative simple past form of each verb. Then use the past forms of the words to write sentences that are true for you.**

	Present	Past	
1	know	knew	My dad knew I was upset about losing the game.
2	leave		
3	find		
4	take		
5	cry		
6	buy		
7	go		
8	get		

B   **Find one error in each question or sentence. Then rewrite it correctly.**

1   How did you lost it?   How did you lose it?

2   I find your keys yesterday.

3   Did you left it behind somewhere?

4   Did he gets his phone back?

5   Someone taked my wallet this morning.

6   Did you tried to find it?

7   I didn't looking for it at school.

8   You drop it under your car yesterday?

3 GRAMMAR AND VOCABULARY

Question words	Verbs	Nouns
who	discover	backpack
what	drop	~~button~~
where	locate	keys
when	return	phone
how	search for	wallet
why	~~fall off~~	your idea:
~~did~~	get back	_____
		your idea:
		_____

A **Write questions in the simple past. Use the ideas in the chart. Add two nouns to the chart.**

1 Excuse me, did this button fall off your sweater?

2 _____

3 _____

4 _____

5 _____

6 _____

7 _____

B **Answer the questions from exercise 3A. Include two negative statements.**

1 Hmm, no, it didn't fall off my sweater. Maybe it fell off the teacher's jacket.

2 _____

3 _____

4 _____

5 _____

6 _____

7 _____

A button

HELP FROM A STRANGER

1 VOCABULARY: Needing and giving help

A Complete each phrase with a word in the box. Write *X* if the phrase does not need another word. Then use the phrases to write sentences that are true for you.

be	be	break	for	~~give~~	lost	of	out

1 _____give_____ a ride
   I gave my friends a ride to the concert.

2 _____ in trouble
   _____

3 _____ down
   _____

4 figure _____
   _____

5 _____ grateful
   _____

6 get _____
   _____

7 show _____
   _____

8 take care _____
   _____

9 feel sorry _____
   _____

10 warn _____
   _____

2 GRAMMAR: Past continuous and simple past

A For each sentence, underline the events that were in progress and circle the interrupting actions. Then complete two more sentences so they are true for you.

1 <u>We were getting on the train</u> when (I dropped my phone.)
2 Last night, I heard a noise while I was brushing my teeth.
3 While I was cooking dinner, the phone rang three times.
4 Jack was helping me with my homework when you came over.
5 When I saw you, you were getting on a bus.
6 While I was _____ last week, _____ .
7 _____ yesterday when _____ .

B **Use the words to make sentences with one event in progress and one interrupting action.**

1   in progress: I / read   interrupting action: James / call

          I was reading   when   *James called*   .

2   in progress: we / study   interrupting action: lights / go out
    While _____ ,
    _____ .

3   interrupting action: I / fall   in progress: I / run for the train
    _____ while
    _____ .

4   in progress: I / shop at the mall   interrupting action: I / find a gift for Tom
    _____ when
    _____ .

5   in progress: I / read a text   interrupting action: I / miss the bus
    While _____ ,
    _____ .

6   in progress: we / driving   interrupting action: the storm / start
    While _____ ,
    _____ .

3   GRAMMAR AND VOCABULARY

A   **Circle the correct phrases to complete the conversations.**

1   **A**   I *was sleeping / slept* on the train when someone *woke me up / was waking me up*
        at the end of the line.

    B   Wow! I bet you *felt sorry for him / were grateful / were in trouble*.

2   **A**   While my nephews *rode / were riding* the roller coaster, it *broke / was breaking*.

    B   Oh no, it sounds like they *felt sorry for him / were grateful / were in trouble*.

3   **A**   I saw your friend *dropped / was dropping* the cake while he *was carrying / carried* it to his girlfriend.

    B   Yeah, we *felt sorry for him / were grateful / were in trouble*.

B   **Complete each sentence. In the first blank, write the correct form of a verb in the box. In the second blank, write your own idea. Remember: use the past continuous, not the simple past, for events that were in progress when something else happened.**

break down	figure out	get lost	give … a ride	~~take care of~~	warn

1   My neighbor went on vacation. I _____*was taking care of*_____ his cat when _____*it ran outside*_____ .

2   Our GPS wasn't working yesterday. We _____ somewhere in Moscow while
    we _____ .

3   I had invitations to two weddings on the same day. When I _____ what to do,
    _____ .

4   I found out there was going to be a big storm. I
    _____ all my neighbors about the storm
    when _____ .

5   I really need a new car. My car _____ while
    I _____ ,

6   I couldn't find my car keys. My sister _____ me
    _____ to work when _____ .

37

YOU'RE KIDDING!

1 FUNCTIONAL LANGUAGE: Giving and reacting to surprising news

A **Complete the conversation with words and phrases in the box. There are two extra words or phrases.**

can't believe	kidding	never guess	not going to
~~real surprise~~	serious	seriously	true

A So, I had a ¹_____real surprise_____ this morning when I was getting ready for class.

B What happened?

A Well, I was watching TV, and you'll ²_____ who I saw.

B Who?

A It was Eduardo from our math class last year.

B You're ³_____ ! Why was he on TV?

A He plays guitar in a band! And they're famous!

B Famous? Are you ⁴_____ ? I didn't even know he was a musician.

A I didn't know either. And you're ⁵_____ believe this. He writes all the songs!

B Wow, that's amazing!

A I know. I ⁶_____ it.

2 REAL-WORLD STRATEGY: Repeating words to express surprise

A **Circle the repeated words that best express surprise.**

1 **A** I'm visiting my sister in Tokyo for the weekend!

    B *In Tokyo?* / *Visiting your sister?*

2 **A** I earned $500 in tips at work today!

    B *At work? / $500?*

3 **A** Rosa was skiing and she broke her leg!

    B *Broke her leg? / Skiing?*

4 **A** I saw an old friend today for the first time in ten years!

    B *An old friend? / Ten years?*

5 **A** Wow, I walked 12 miles yesterday.

    B *Twelve miles? / Yesterday?*

3 FUNCTIONAL LANGUAGE AND REAL-WORLD STRATEGY

A Respond to each piece of surprising news. Use an expression for reacting with surprise and repeated words.

1 A You'll never guess who I saw when I was shopping today! I saw Angelina Jolie!

B *Angelina Jolie? Are you serious?*

A Yes! It was so exciting. But I lost my phone, so I couldn't take a picture.

2 A You're not going to believe this. I found a diamond ring in the park when I was running this morning.

B _____

A Yeah, but I think I'm going to take it to the police station.

3 A I had a real surprise this morning. Remember the ring I lost last year? I found it in a jar of pickles!

B _____

A Yes, it was so funny.

4 A I can't believe it. I had such a hard time this semester, but I got As in all of my classes.

B _____

A Uh-huh, I feel so good about it!

5 A You're not going to believe this. Someone took my wallet when I was at the police station.

B _____

A Yeah, I was shocked. The police were really helpful, though.

B Write short conversations about surprising things that happened to you. Include expressions for giving surprising news, expressions for reacting with surprise, and repeated words. You can use the ideas given or your own ideas.

saw someone you knew a long time ago	found something valuable	won a game or contest

Conversation 1
A _____
B _____

Conversation 2
A _____
B _____

Conversation 3
A _____
B _____

STORYTELLING

1 READING

A **READ FOR DETAIL** Read Anna's story. Then read the statements and check (✓) *True*, *False*, or *Not given*.

When I was young, I was afraid of the dark, so I always slept with a small table lamp on. One night, I couldn't sleep. I got out of bed and went to the kitchen to get a glass of water. When I came back into my room, I stepped on something. As I fell onto the floor, the glass of water flew out of my hand, and the light went out. It was so dark and I was so scared. I was sure that there was a monster in my room and that I stepped on its foot! I screamed and screamed. My parents came running into the room to see what was wrong. By then I was crying and I couldn't really talk. My father turned my bedroom light on, and my mother picked me up off the floor and put me into my bed. After I calmed down, I said that a monster turned my lamp off when I stepped on its foot. Then my father bent over and picked something up. It was a stuffed animal! I tripped on it and accidentally unplugged the lamp as I fell down! We all laughed and laughed about it. Then my parents plugged my lamp back in and cleaned all the water off my floor.

		True	False	Not given
1	The writer was afraid of the dark.	☐	☐	☐
2	She couldn't sleep because she was afraid.	☐	☐	☐
3	When the light went out, she got back into bed.	☐	☐	☐
4	Her parents came in when they heard her screaming.	☐	☐	☐
5	She fell because she stepped on some water.	☐	☐	☐

2 LISTENING

A 🔊 5.01 Listen to two people discussing the story in exercise 1A. Then answer the questions.

1 What does Karen think of Anna's story?

2 Which of the four *S*s does Karen think Anna did not include?

3 How does Karen think Anna should change her story?

4 What did Karen think Anna stepped on in the story?

3 WRITING

A **Write a short story like the one in exercise 1A. It can be true or you can make it up. Remember the four *Ss*: *simple*; *shared experiences*; *show, don't tell*; and *surprise*.**

When I was young, I was afraid of _____ , so I always _____

_____

_____

_____

_____

_____

_____

_____

_____

_____

_____

_____

_____

_____

_____

CHECK AND REVIEW

Read the statements. Can you do these things?

UNIT 5	Mark the boxes. ☑ I can do it. ? I am not sure. I can …	If you are not sure, go back to these pages in the Student's Book.
VOCABULARY	☐ use verbs for losing and finding things. ☐ use verbs for needing and giving help.	page 44 page 46
GRAMMAR	☐ use the simple past. ☐ use the past continuous and the simple past.	page 45 page 47
FUNCTIONAL LANGUAGE	☐ give and react to surprising news. ☐ repeat words to express surprise.	page 48 page 49
SKILLS	☐ write a short story. ☐ use storytelling expressions.	page 51 page 51

6.1 MOVING TO A MEGACITY

1 VOCABULARY: Urban problems

A **Use the clues to complete the crossword puzzle.**

ACROSS

3 Factories can cause _____ in the water.

5 Old candy wrappers and used tissues are _____ .

7 We all want to breathe clean _____ .

8 If something burns, it makes _____ .

9 A picture spray-painted on the wall of a building
is called _____ .

DOWN

1 There is not a lot of open _____ in big cities.
It's all covered by buildings and roads.

2 Sidewalks are made of _____ .

4 In a _____ , cars move very slowly or not at all.

5 There is a lot of _____ on the roads when
everyone is on their way to work.

6 Big cities are not usually quiet – there is a lot
of _____ .

8 City apartments are usually small because there
isn't a lot of _____ for big apartments.

Crossword grid, 3 ACROSS: p o l l u t i o n

2 GRAMMAR: Quantifiers

A **Put each word in the box in the correct place in the chart.**

~~air~~	car	graffiti	noise	road	space	train
~~building~~	concrete	highway	office	sidewalk	traffic	trash
bus	color	land	pollution	smoke	traffic jam	tree

Count nouns	Noncount nouns
building	air

B **Correct the sentences.**

1   There are so ~~much~~ ^{many} people in this city.

2   Almost all of the peoples here live in apartments.

3   There is very few space left for new people.

4   There is almost no trashes on the streets in my neighborhood.

5   Several of the building downtown have graffiti on them.

6   There is so many graffiti on the building where I work.

7   Almost no of the real color of the building shows.

3 GRAMMAR AND VOCABULARY

A **Write sentences with quantifiers about the place where you live. Use three count nouns and three noncount nouns from exercise 2A.**

1   *There are so few tall buildings in my hometown.*

2   _____

3   _____

4   _____

5   _____

6   _____

7   _____

1 VOCABULARY: Adverbs of manner

A **Choose all of the adverbs that you can use with each verb or verb phrase.**

1 speak

☐ angrily   ☐ completely   ☐ politely
☐ clearly   ☐ loudly   ☐ safely

2 drive

☐ angrily   ☐ correctly   ☐ loudly
☐ clearly   ☐ dangerously   ☐ safely

3 play the piano

☐ beautifully   ☐ correctly   ☐ loudly
☐ completely   ☐ dangerously   ☐ safely

4 explain something

☐ calmly   ☐ completely   ☐ politely
☐ clearly   ☐ correctly   ☐ safely

5 answer a question

☐ calmly   ☐ completely   ☐ dangerously
☐ clearly   ☐ correctly   ☐ politely

2 GRAMMAR: Present and future real conditionals

A **Circle the correct words to complete the sentences.**

1 If there *won't be / aren't* any trash cans in the city, people *will throw / throw* their garbage on the street.

2 When there *is / will be* a lot of trash on the street, a city *looks / will look* ugly.

3 The city *looks / will look* great in the summer *if / when* we clean it up now.

4 When it *is / will be* hot outside, the trash *starts / starting* to smell bad.

5 People *move / will move* away if we *will take / don't take* care of our city.

6 If the city *will get / gets* more polluted than it is now, visitors *don't want / won't want* to come here.

7 If we *are keeping / keep* our parks clean, more people *will go / go* to them.

8 When lots of people *use / will use* a public space, the city usually *is spending / spends* more money to maintain it.

9 Musicians *will come / are coming* to perform concerts in a park if it *will be / is* clean, popular, and beautiful.

A **Match the sentence halves. Then write _P_ after the present real sentences and _F_ after the future real sentences.**

1 If you don't write clearly, ___b___

2 If you speak angrily, _____

3 If you drive safely, _____

4 If you drive dangerously, _____

5 If you answer the test questions completely, _____

6 If you speak politely, _____

7 If people play their music loudly, _____

a you will probably get an A on the test. _____

b the teacher won't be able to read your writing. ___F___

c people will want to listen to you. _____

d no one wants to hear what you have to say. _____

e you might injure yourself or someone else. _____

f their neighbors get upset. _____

g you don't have accidents. _____

B **Change the _if_ clauses from exercise 3A to express the opposite idea. Then write new results.**

1 _If you write clearly, your classmates will be able to follow your notes._

2 _____

3 _____

4 _____

5 _____

6 _____

7 _____

C **Complete the sentences. Use present real or future real conditionals and adverbs of manner.**

1 Children _____
if they ask _____ .

2 In my city, people _____
when they ride bikes _____ .

3 Other passengers _____
if someone is not speaking _____
on the bus.

4 When people explain problems
_____ , it is easier to
_____ .

5 If I speak _____ ,
my co-workers _____
my presentation.

1   FUNCTIONAL LANGUAGE: Expressing concern and relief

A   **Complete the conversations with the sentences in the boxes.**

Conversation 1

> Are you all right?   What a relief!   Is anything wrong?

A   1 _____

B   I had a terrible night last night. My apartment building caught on fire.

A   Oh no! 2 _____

B   Yeah, the fire was pretty bad, but I'm OK. My neighbors are all right, too.

A   3 _____

Conversation 2

> That's such a relief!   I'm glad to hear that.   I was really worried.   Is everyone OK?

A   Hey, I heard there was an earthquake near you last night. 4 _____

B   Thanks for calling. Yeah, we're all OK.

A   5 _____ Did your house get damaged?

B   No, it's fine. A few things fell off of shelves, but that's all.

A   6 _____ 7 _____

2   REAL-WORLD STRATEGY: Using *though* to give a contrasting idea

A   **Add *though* to the sentences where it is appropriate. Remember to include a comma.**

                 , though

1   No one got hurt. It was scary. ⌃

2   I fell on the beach and hurt my arm. I didn't break it. The sand was soft.

3   My car broke down on the highway. It doesn't have any major problems. It just ran out of gas.

4   The fire was really bad. The whole building burned down. No one was hurt.

5   There was a huge accident on the highway. We were stuck in traffic for two hours. We had a good conversation in the car.

6   I missed my bus this morning. I got to work on time. My friend saw me at the bus stop and gave me a ride.

B **Imagine that you are describing the situations to someone. Write sentences with _though_.**

1 Your bus crashed. You all had to stay on the bus for an hour. No one was hurt.

My bus crashed, and we all had to stay on the bus for an hour. No one was hurt, though.

2 You fell on an icy sidewalk. You scratched your leg. You didn't break it.

_____

3 You cut your hand. It looked bad. You didn't have to go to the hospital.

_____

4 A lot of people got sick from eating bad shrimp at your office party. You didn't get sick. You didn't have any shrimp.

_____

5 You got lost on your vacation. You had a great time. You met some nice people.

_____

3 FUNCTIONAL LANGUAGE AND REAL-WORLD STRATEGY

A **Put the conversations in order.**

Conversation 1

B I'm fine. My bike is broken, though.   _____

A That's a relief.   _____

B Yeah, I just need to buy some new parts.   _____

A Are you all right? I heard you had a bicycle accident.   _____

A Oh no! Can you fix it?   _____

Conversation 2

B Why? What happened?   _____

A I saw an ambulance in front of your house today. Is anything wrong?   _____

B No, we're fine.   _____

A None of us was hurt. The ambulance driver is in trouble, though.   _____

B He drove to the wrong house!   _____

A What a relief! I was really worried.   _____

B **Complete the conversation with _though_ and expressions of concern and relief.**

A ¹_____ Lee saw you at the hospital today. ²_____

B Thanks, I'm fine. I was just visiting my sister.

A ³_____ But I hope your sister is OK.

B She was really sick. She's feeling a lot better now, ⁴_____ .

A ⁵_____

BEATING THE TRAFFIC

1 LISTENING

A 🔊 **6.01** **LISTEN FOR DETAIL** **Listen to the podcast. Choose the correct answers.**

1 What is the podcast about?
    a self-driving cars   **b** underwater cars   **c** flying cars

2 What is Teresa designing a car for?
    a emergencies   **b** entertainment   **c** to solve traffic problems

3 Does she think everyone will have one of these cars?
    a Yes.   **b** No.   **c** She's not sure.

4 When does Teresa think we will have these cars?
    a in a few years   **b** in several years   **c** never

B 🔊 **6.01** **Read each line from the podcast. Who said it? Check (✓)**
   Steve or *Teresa*. **Then listen to the podcast again to check your answers.**

		Steve	Teresa
1	A lot of sci-fi movies show people driving around in the sky.	☐	☐
2	My goal is to develop flying cars for emergencies.	☐	☐
3	… do you think flying cars will solve our traffic problems?	☐	☐
4	Can you tell us why?	☐	☐
5	Flying ambulances won't have that problem.	☐	☐
6	We still have a lot of work to do …	☐	☐

2 READING

A **Read the comment by a podcast listener, Opinionzzz. Check (✓) the problems that he writes about.**
   Circle the ones that Steve and Teresa already mentioned.

Opinionzzz wrote:

I hope we never have flying cars of any kind. I think even flying ambulances are a bad idea. Why? Well, first of all, if everyone is flying cars in the sky, we'll have traffic jams in the air! And imagine a car accident in the air – flying car parts might fall onto people on the ground. People in the flying cars might even fall out!

Second, we already have a lot of air pollution. I think that flying cars would create more of it. The air in big cities would be horrible.

Third, cars break down all the time. When your car breaks down, you just pull over to the side of the road. What will you do if your car breaks down in the air? Your car would probably just fall to the ground. That might destroy your car and even hurt someone else … or worse.

I definitely don't think we should have flying cars. Let's find other ways to get ambulances to people more quickly.

☐ flying too fast   ☐ falling out of the sky
☐ traffic in the sky   ☐ too much noise
☐ expensive cost of cars   ☐ air pollution
☐ cars breaking down   ☐ being afraid of flying

A Write your own comment responding to Steve's podcast and Opinionzzz's comment. Decide if you think flying ambulances are a good idea or not. Give reasons and use questions to make points.

CHECK AND REVIEW

Read the statements. Can you do these things?

UNIT 6	Mark the boxes. ☑ I can do it. ? I am not sure. I can …	If you are not sure, go back to these pages in the Student's Book.
VOCABULARY	☐ use nouns to talk about urban problems. ☐ use adverbs of manner.	page 54 page 56
GRAMMAR	☐ use quantifiers. ☐ use present and future real conditionals.	page 55 page 57
FUNCTIONAL LANGUAGE	☐ express concern and relief. ☐ use *though* to give a contrasting idea.	page 58 page 59
SKILLS	☐ write a post giving your point of view. ☐ use questions to make points.	page 61 page 61

EXTRA ACTIVITIES

1.5 TIME TO SPEAK What makes a leader?

A   **Decide if you would or would not like to be a leader – for example, a leader of your school or of your country.**

- Make a list of the good things about being a leader.
- Make a list of the difficult things a leader has to do.
- Decide whether being a leader is mostly good or mostly bad.

B   **Make an audio recording about the good and bad things about being a leader. End your recording with your decision about whether it is mostly good or mostly bad to be a leader.**

C   **Bring your recording to class and listen to your classmates' recordings. How many of you think being a leader is mostly a good thing? How many of you think it is mostly bad?**

2.5 TIME TO SPEAK Things to bring

A   **Imagine that someone has an item that you really want, but they won't take money for it. They will only exchange it for something that is very important to you. Write a description of the thing you will exchange.**

B   **Bring your description (and, if possible, your item or a picture of your item) to class. Talk with your classmates, showing your items and sharing your descriptions. Then exchange your description for the description of something that you would like to have.**

3.5 TIME TO SPEAK Secret spots

A   **Research secret spots in a city that you have visited or would like to visit.**

- Search for "secret spots in [city]."
- Write down three secret spots that look interesting to you.
- Take notes on where each spot is and what you can do there.
- Print out a map of the city and mark the spots on your map.
- Find out how to get from each spot to the next.
- Write directions from one spot to the next spot to the next.

B   **Make a video of yourself giving a presentation about the secret spots. In your video:**

- Show the spots on your map.
- Describe each spot.
- Explain how to get from one spot to the next.

4.5 TIME TO SPEAK Microadventures

A **Think of an idea for a microadventure that you could go on with friends. Go online and research it.**

  - Write detailed notes about what the microadventure involves (where it is, how you could get there, what you could do there, how long it would take, and who you could go with).

  - Make a list of pros (or benefits) of the microadventure.

  - Make a list of cons (or possible problems) of the microadventure.

B **Invite your class on the microadventure. Use your notes to tell them all about it. How many of your classmates would like to go on your microadventure? What are their reasons for going or not going?**

5.5 TIME TO SPEAK Believe it or not …

A **Go online and find a surprising story about something that was lost and then found years later. Or, tell a surprising personal lost-and-found story.**

  - Take notes on the story.

  - Write the story in your own words.

  - Add one detail to the story that is made up (it didn't really happen).

  - Make an audio recording of your story.

B **Bring your recording to class. Listen to each other's recordings. Guess which detail of each story is made up.**

6.5 TIME TO SPEAK If everyone plants something, …

A **Go online and research creative ways to save energy or cut down on pollution. Choose one idea to focus on.**

  - Take notes on the idea.

  - Write three reasons explaining how the idea will help solve a problem.

  - Make a poster to illustrate your idea and highlight its benefits.

B **Bring your poster to class and present the idea to your classmates. Ask your classmates to discuss its benefits and possible problems. Then ask them to decide if they want to use the idea.**

The authors and publishers acknowledge the following sources of copyright material and are grateful for the permissions granted. While every effort has been made, it has not always been possible to identify the sources of all the material used, or to trace all copyright holders. If any omissions are brought to our notice, we will be happy to include the appropriate acknowledgements on reprinting and in the next update to the digital edition, as applicable.

Photographs
Key: B = Below, BR = Below Right, CL = Centre Left, CR = Centre Right, TR = Top Right.

All the photographs are sourced from Getty Images.

p. 2, p. 83: PeopleImages/E+; p. 3: KidStock/Blend Images; p. 4: Leon Bennett/WireImage; p. 5 (BR): andresr/E+; p. 5 (TR): Topic Images Inc./Alloy; p. 6: Maskot; p. 7, p. 71: LeoPatrizi/E+; p. 8: fstop123/E+; p. 9 (CL): J.M.F. Almeida/Moment; p. 9 (CR): Tuul & Bruno Morandi/ Photolibrary; p. 11: delihayat/E+; p. 13: martin-dm/iStock/Getty Images Plus; p. 14: Klaus Vedfelt/DigitalVision; p. 15: carterdayne/E+; p. 16: Hannah Foslien/Getty Images Sport; p. 18: aaaaimages/Moment; p. 19: DarthArt/iStock/Getty Images Plus; p. 20: Images By Tang Ming Tung/DigitalVision; p. 21: Martin Polsson/Maskot; p. 22: kitthanes/ iStock/Getty Images Plus; p. 23: Siri Stafford/DigitalVision; p. 24, p. 54, p. 85: Hero Images; p. 26: Zero Creatives/Cultura; p. 27: Ariel Skelley/ DigitalVision; p. 29: Radius Images; p. 30: Adam Gault/OJO Images; p. 31: Shah Saad/EyeEm; p. 35: Shah Saad/EyeEm; p. 36: Trinette Reed/ Blend Images; p. 37: Andreas Kirsch/EyeEm; p. 38: xavierarnau/E+; p. 39: LightFieldStudios/iStock/Getty Images Plus; p. 41: JLPH/Cultura; p. 42: David Crespo/Moment; p. 44: Dave and Les Jacobs/Blend Images; p. 45 (TR): Jeffrey Coolidge/Corbis/Getty Images Plus; p. 45 (BR): Adrian Weinbrecht/Cultura/Getty Images Plus; p. 47: Dawid Garwol/ EyeEm; p. 48: petrovv/iStock/Getty Images Plus; p. 49: Ashley Cooper/ Corbis Documentary.

Front cover photography by Alija/E+.

Audio production by CityVox, New York.

Corpus
Development of this publication has made use of the Cambridge English Corpus (CEC). The CEC is a multi-billion word collection of contemporary spoken and written English. It includes British English, American English, and other varieties. It also includes the Cambridge Learner Corpus, the world's biggest collection of learner writing, developed in collaboration with Cambridge Assessment. Cambridge University Press uses the CEC to provide evidence about language use that helps to produce better language teaching materials.

Our Evolve authors study the Corpus to see how English is really used, and to identify typical learner mistakes. This information informs the authors' selection of vocabulary, grammar items and Student's Book Corpus features such as the Accuracy Check, Register Check, and Insider English.